Trees of Newport

on the estates of the
Preservation Society of Newport County

by Richard L. Champlin

Published in cooperation with
**THE PRESERVATION SOCIETY
OF NEWPORT COUNTY**
Newport, Rhode Island

APPLEWOOD BOOKS
Bedford, Massachusetts

Published in part from a grant by the
Firestone Foundation, Akron, Ohio

Thank you for purchasing an Applewood book. Applewood reprints America's lively classics—books from the past that are still of interest to modern readers. For a free copy of our current catalog, write to:

Applewood Books
P.O. Box 365
Bedford, MA 01730

ISBN 1-55709-962-6

This booklet sets about the pleasurable task of enumerating and describing the trees on six of the estates owned by the Preservation Society of Newport County. Because of their transient nature, most shrubs have been omitted.

The mansions on these estates range in date of construction from 1839 when Kingscote was built to 1902 when Rosecliff came into existence. Between these dates even the styles of landscaping underwent changes, so that Chateau-sur-Mer (1852), Marble House (1892), The Breakers (1895), and The Elms (1901) were confronted with new and wider selections of plant material, as well as changing tastes. The end product, as seen by today's visitor, differs from what the first owners of the estates saw, but the results now are as fully rewarding.

The gardens of the Newport estates, no less than the mansions themselves, required teams of workers to prune and manicure, to trim and primp the grounds. Troops of gardeners and their helpers daily set off to work down Bellevue Avenue armed with their weaponry of hoes, rakes, spades, and pitchforks, some turning in at one estate, some at another. In its heyday, and even as late as the 1940s, Chateau-sur-Mer employed eleven gardeners, the chief gardener at the Wetmore estate for thirty years being a Scot, John Cairns.

To visualize what awaited them, conjure up pictures of formal gardens, of fountains and pools, of neat shrubbery and graceful trees. The gardens have largely passed now, the fountains have dried up, but the trees remain. In fact, those trees that have survived the storms - and regrettably many have succumbed - look grander now than when the estates were young, more thrifty, more mature. Old photographs of the newly erected estates depict them as raw and stark, because of the newness of their plantings, thus justifying Henry James when he described the cottages as "white elephants".

The newest tree imports from China and Japan, Greece and Algeria, Turkey and Scotland mustered in on the lawns at Newport, trees that had been sought out by such globe-trotters as Ernest "Chinese" Wilson, who with the Veitches, and others of their day, sent their latest finds in the Orient to Charles Sprague Sargent at the Arnold Arboretum outside of Boston for propagation and trial. Once the stock became available on the market, such Newport dealers as Samuel Smith, Michael Butler, William Maher, as well as Fadden & Henderson, and Galvin & Geraghty purveyed them to the summer colonists.

At first only the wealthy could afford these rare and exotic trees, just as only they could own cars and telephones, yet through the general democratization of things the exotics, especially the newer varieties of them, have become commonplace. Japanese Maples grow on many street corners today, and even trailer homes may have Colorado Blue Spruce standing beside them. What the trees on the Newport estates do excel in, however, is their unchallenged seniority. One must roam far and wide to find a London Plane Tree as massive and venerable as the one at Chateau-sur-Mer with its seven foot trunk diameter.

By far the most frequently planted trees to be found on all six of the Preservation Society's estates are the Norway and Sycamore Maples, the London Plane Tree, and the European Beech in one or more of its varieties. A veteran nurseryman, Cornelius Hoogendorn, commented that he had invited his fellow nurserymen from all over the country to Newport to view the trees. They enthused most over the Beeches on the estates and elsewhere in Newport. He observed that Newport's climate, soil, and moisture favor beeches as do few other places.

If the estates hold some species in common, each also has trees unique to it. The Bald Cypress grows only at the Breakers, the Bottle Brush Buckeye only at Chateau-sur-Mer, and so on. While not all the trees were planted at once, and replacements of old ones past their usefulness were made from time to time, it is known that no new plantings were made at Chateau-sur-Mer after 1940.

Landscape gardening had come into flower during the late years of the last century. Frederick Law Olmsted, who left his mark on Newport's Ocean Drive, Morton Park, and numerous estates, directed the landscaping at Chateau-sur-Mer. His firm, after his death, laid out the grounds at The Breakers. At the Elms Jacques Greber designed the plantings. Writing in *Garden and Forest*, Mrs. Schuyler Van Rensselaer, after surveying the work of professional landscapers in Newport, applauded the results as "gardenesque". And in these later times even the most casual observer can, too. Because of their vision, Newport has become one vast arboretum.

The Trees

1. Arborvitae - *Thuja occidentalis*

Source - Northeastern North America
Location -
The Breakers, Chateau-sur-Mer, The Elms
Height - to 50 ft.   Cones - 1/2 in.

Evergreens and fragrance go together. In the Arborvitae, or just plain Cedar as most people call it, fragrance reaches an all-time high. Think of Robert Frost,

> ". . . half boring through, half climbing through
> A swamp of cedar. Choked with oil of cedar. . ."
> ("An Encounter")

Of all the trees taken by early explorers from North America back to Europe, Arborvitae heads the list. Jacques Cartier found it in the St. Lawrence Valley in 1535-36 and promptly introduced it in Paris, an early instance of transplanting from North America.

Many cedars develop trunks twisted like a corkscrew. Why? Some say owls perch on the tops of young trees on moonlight nights facing the moon all night long. They follow it as it arches from horizon to horizon, and the tree keeps on reeling ever after.

2. Ash, European - *Fraxinus excelsior*

Source - Europe, North Africa
Location - The Breakers, Chateau-sur-Mer
Height - to 140 ft.   Leaves - 10 to 12 in.

Both ashes and hickories have compound leaves, that is, leaves composed of smaller leaflets arranged oppositely along a central stem. But in ashes the leaves themselves and the buds grow opposite each other along the twigs, unlike the hickories which have alternate parts. Further, the European Ash, much planted in Europe as an ornamental tree, has jet black buds late in the growing season and all winter, which distinguish it from any North American Ash.

Formerly the branches of this tree went into the making of barrel hoops.

3. Beech, European
Fagus sylvatica

Source - Europe
Location - The Breakers, Chateau-sur-Mer,
The Elms, Kingscote, Marble House, Rosecliff
Height - to 80 ft.   Leaves - 4 in.   Bur - 1 in.

In England, where this tree abounds, peasants
of Robin Hood's time were allowed to gather its
branches from forests of the noblemen for fuel.
Although not permitted to fell the trees, they could
take fallen branches or any limbs on the tree
reached with a hook or shepherd's crook. Hence
the expression "by hook or by crook".

With its smooth, gray bark, the Beech makes
an ideal witness tree and commits to memory many
a pair of initials, along with dates, hearts, and
cupid's arrows. However these tree tattoos are in-
delible. They have been known to last for centuries.

The tree has many varieties: the Purple, or
Copper, Beech (*Fagus sylvatica atropunicea*), the
Weeping Beech (*Fagus sylvatica pendula*), and
the Fernleaf Beech (*Fagus sylvatica laciniata*).
The Fernleaf Beech reaches a peak of excellence
in Newport; no finer or more venerable specimen
to be found anywhere in America than that at
Redwood Library, a tree known to have been
planted there in 1835.

4. Birch, European - *Betula pendula*

Source - Europe, Asia Minor
Location - The Breakers
Height - to 60 ft.   Leaves - to 2 1/2 in.

This tree grows at The Breakers along with its
variety *gracilis*, which displays finely dissected
leaves. This detail, along with the somewhat
weeping form of the branchlets, gives the tree
an airy, graceful appearance. The white trunk
lightens up the dark corner of any garden. Not
immune to insect pests, the European Birch has
an all-too-short life span.

5. Birch, Paper - *Betula papyrifera*

Source - Northern North America
Location - Chateau-sur-Mer, Kingscote
Height - to 80 ft.   Leaves - to 4 in.

Also called White Birch and Canoe Birch, this tree
excels in whiteness. The Paper Birch, native to
Canada and the northern tier of states including
Rhode Island, can be told from the Gray Birch by
its chalky white bark. Gray Birch has smooth bark.
European Birch, also with white bark, has drooping twigs.

It has served in countless ways - canoes for
the Indians, batons for conductors, ferrules for
schoolmasters, snowshoes for travelers.

Ripping the bark off for souvenirs usually leaves
an ugly gash too deep to turn white again. Hence
the rule: don't peel the bark of a living tree.

6. Box - *Buxus sempervirens*

Source - Europe, North Africa, Western Asia
Location -
Chateau-sur-Mer, The Elms, Kingscote, Rosecliff
Height - to 25 ft.   Leaves - to 1 in.

Hedgerows of Box in formal gardens can be made to obey the whim of the one clipping them. This shrub, together with Privet and Yew, is suitable for the topiary art. In hot weather its foliage possesses a distinct pungence.

Turners, cabinet-makers, wood engravers, and carvers all make use of Boxwood. Being yellow, dense, hard, and heavy, the wood is one of the few timbers sold by weight instead of volume.

Box lives up to its name *sempervirens* by being long-lived. One hundred and fifty year old specimens occur at Mt. Vernon.

7. Buckeye, Bottlebrush
Aesculus parviflora

Source - Southeastern United States
Location - Chateau-sur-Mer
Height - to 15 ft.   Leaves - to 12 in.

William Bartram, an early American botanist, first
discovered the Bottlebrush Buckeye in the Tennessee Valley. The common name, Bottlebrush,
refers to the long spikes of white flowers arranged
like bristles on all sides of the stalks. A mid-season
bloomer, this shrub from the deep South withstands New England winters readily. It develops
a mound of branches and shoots that spread wider
each year. Being a Buckeye, it has as near rela-
tives the Horse Chestnut and the Sweet Buckeye
of Ohio fame.

8. Cedar, Atlas - *Cedrus atlantica glauca*

Source -
North Africa, the Atlas Mountains of Algeria
Location - The Breakers
Height - to 120 ft. Needles - to 1 in. Cones - to 3 in.

From the Atlas Mountains of North Africa to
Newport comes the Atlantic Cedar, close relative
of the biblical Cedar of Lebanon. This represents
a descent from 2000 foot elevations to near sea
level, yet this cedar takes it in stride. Trees in Algeria reportedly have trunk diameters of 4 1/2 to
6 feet, with tier over tier of nearly horizontal branches. The shading of blue-green-silver catches the
eye at any season. Egg-shaped cones sit upright
on the branches and require at least two seasons
to mature. Then they fall apart a scale at a time,
sometimes found on the ground below. Only rarely
does a whole cone tumble.

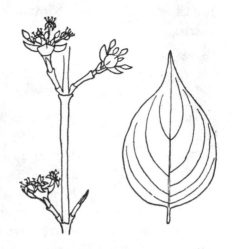

9. Cherry, Cornelian - *Cornus mas*

Source - Southern Europe, the Orient
Location - Chateau-sur-Mer
Height - to 20 ft.   Leaves - to 2 1/2 in.

Only the early-season visitors to Chateau-sur-Mer
will see the Cornelian Cherry at its best. Not a
true cherry, but a dogwood, it blooms even before
the Forsythia, having twigs completely wreathed
with tiny yellow flowers. It leads the procession
of trees and shrubs that blossom before leafing
out. Scarlet, gem-like fruit follows later in the
season, fruit that is edible and has been used in
preserves.

10. Cherry, Japanese Flowering
Prunus serrulata

Source - China, Korea, Japan
Location - Chateau-sur-Mer, Kingscote
Height - to 25 ft.   Leaves - to 6 in.

Describing the flowering cherries, A. E. Housman burst into poetry:

"Loveliest of trees, the cherry now
 Is hung with bloom along the bough."

His trees were white, whereas most are shades of pink, and they come in double or single forms.

A symbol of this country's friendship with Japan, the Japanese Flowering Cherry seems well suited to the Newport that gave birth to Matthew Calbraith Perry, celebrated as the American who opened the trade routes to Japan.

11. Cherry, Sweet - *Prunus avium*

Source - Europe
Location - Kingscote
Height - to 75 ft.   Leaves - to 6 in.

Hardly a match for cultivated cherries, the fruit of this Cherry appeals somewhat to humans and very much to birds - hence the name *avium* (of birds). Found growing around old homesteads and escaped from there to roadsides, it often accompanies the Mulberry, and not just by chance. Farmers knew that they would never get to pick the cherries if the birds found them first, so they planted mulberries alongside their cherry to distract the birds with berries that ripen at the same time and lure the birds away from the more desirable cherries.

The ash gray trunk of this Sweet (or Mazzard) Cherry would be smooth except for the raised streaks arranged horizontally around the tree.

12. Coffee Tree, Kentucky
Gymnocladus dioicus

Source - Central United States
Location - Chateau-sur-Mer
Height - to 60 ft.   Leaves - to 3 ft.

Despite its very large leaves, compounded of many small leaflets, the Kentucky Coffee Tree casts a thin shade. In spring this tree gets off to a slow start. The twigs which have looked the next thing to dead all winter, finally leaf out after other species have full-grown leaves. It made a name for itself in Kentucky where first the Indians and later the Whites used its bean-like seeds for coffee. The beans grow in flat pods resembling narrow Lima Beans, only they are dark brown or black and hang on the tree into the winter months.

The durable wood of this tree has served as fence posts and railroad ties, and though coarse-grained, it takes a high polish.

13. Cork Tree - *Phellodendron lavallei*

Source - Japan
Location - Chateau-sur-Mer
Height - to 45 ft.   Leaves - 10 to 15 in.

Patterned bark distinguishes the Cork Tree, bark
that raises high, light ridges with dark troughs
running helter-skelter between them. As an
ornamental tree, it shows to best advantage in
the winter. Its bark is no match for that of the
cork-producing oaks, although attempts have
been made to use it.

The compound, pinnate leaves when crushed
have a strong aroma, as do the dark berries, which
hang on well into the winter.

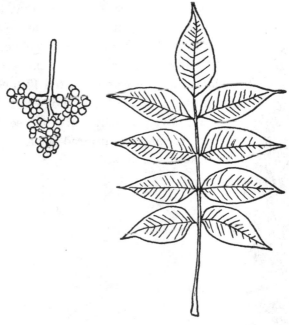

14. Cryptomeria - *Cryptomeria japonica*

Source - Japan
Location -
The Breakers, Chateau-sur-Mer, Marble House
Height - to 125 ft.   Needles - 1/2 to 1 in.

For timber the Japanese plant this species more
than any other tree, and they use not only the
wood for many purposes, but the bark for roofing.
They have so done for centuries, valuing every
specimen of it until now it is known only in cultivation, not in the wild.

As a transplant, we find it a dark, somber
tree, that swallows up the sunlight. But on its
native soil it becomes a grand monarch, compar-
able to the Sequoias of this country. In the 1890s
Charles S. Sargent found an avenue of Crypto-
merias leading from Nikko to Tokyo. According
to tradition, the first trees of this avenue were
planted by a poor man in the 17th century in
memory of the founder of the Tokugawa
dynasty. This double row of trees is a living
memorial, since injured or dead ones are re-
placed with new.

15. Cypress, Bald - *Taxodium distichum*

Source - Southern and Central United States
Location - The Breakers
Height - to 150 ft.   Needles - 1/2 to 3/4 in.

The dry lawn of The Breakers contrasts sharply with the usual habitat of Bald Cypress, namely the mucky swamps of the South. There it develops "knees" to aid its breathing, knees that rise as much as five feet out of the water. Hollow knees have been used as beehives, and the wood of the tree itself resists decay, rendering it valuable in wet uses, such as for house gutters. In the South Bald Cypress plays host to Spanish moss and certain tree-growing orchids.

When is an evergreen not an evergreen? Bald Cypress and Larch trees, unlike most other conifers, lose their needles in the winter and look the nearest thing to dead. But in the summer the shimmery, feather-like foliage of the Bald Cypress redeems it.

16. Cypress, Hinoki - *Chamaecyparis obtusa*

Source - Japan
Location - The Breakers, Chateau-sur-Mer
Height - to 100 ft.   Cones - 1/2 in.

This tree finds uses in Japan that range from serving as the sacred tree of Shinto temple plantings, to being a valuable timber tree, to rating as the most choice wood for the famous lacquered art objects, to making an ideal dwarf for potted tree culture - the art of bonsai. From a woodworker's viewpoint, the fact that its wood takes a high polish is recommendation enough.

Hinoki Cypress exclusively goes into the building of Shinto temples. In plantations it stands 100 feet high, old specimens having no branches for the first 50 or 60 feet. But not all trees reach that height. The variety called *nana* is a dwarf.

Rhode Island's Dr. George Rogers Hall first introduced the Hinoki Cypress to this country in 1861.

17. Cypress, Sawara
Chamaecyparis pisifera

Source - Japan
Location - The Breakers, Kingscote
Height - to 100 ft.   Cones - 1/2 in.

Like the Hinoki Cypress, the Sawara makes a valuable timber tree in Japan. As a result of long cultivation, it has produced many forms and varieties, some of which were formerly known as retinosporas.

The more ragged crown, with looser and more upright branches in this species contrasts with the rounder top and more pendulous branches of the Hinoki.

Much planted in this country, the Sawara Cypress was first introduced in 1861 to England.

18. Dogwood - *Cornus florida*

Source - Eastern United States
Location - Chateau-sur-Mer, Kingscote
Height - to 40 ft.   Leaves 2 to 5 in.

The state tree of Virginia, Dogwood enhances
the landscape of any state where it grows. In
Rhode Island the typical white form occurs as
an understory tree at the edge of woods. Sometimes called Yankee Boxwood here, it has served
in the making of weavers' shuttles, golf club
heads, and wooden fold-up rules. Its biggest asset
by far, though, is its early, glamorous flowering.
The pink form, *Cornus florida rubra,* which occurs
at both Chateau-sur-Mer and Kingscote, caused
a tempest in a teapot. Dealers sent out fliers pic-
turing it in color. Buyers disbelieved. It couldn't
be that pink, they said. But the dealers offered
to hold a colored illustration alongside a tree. The
dealers won.

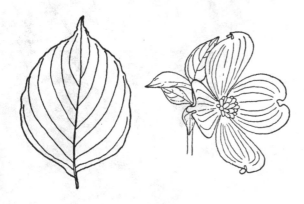

*Despite its nearness to the sea, The Breakers
displays a rich variety of vigorous trees, all of
which must withstand salt spray and buffeting
by sea winds.*

19. Elm, American - *Ulmus americana*

Source - Central and Eastern North America
Location -
Chateau-sur-Mer, Kingscote, Marble House
Height - to 120 ft. Leaves - to 6 in. Seeds - 1/2 in.

Can the American Elm be saved? Work goes on
currently to find the elm most resistant to disease.
Already its disappearance one by one has altered
the landscape. In former days lofty elms presided
over New England villages, lending a reposeful
air. In some instances the spreading tops on either
side met over the middle of the street creating
a leafy arch. On better specimens the columnar
trunk surges up to great height, then like a foun-
tain sprays out in fine streamers on all sides. The
generation that missed these sights has missed a
treat. And the nesting orioles miss the elms, too.

The estate named for this stately tree, that is
The Elms, has now lost its last specimen of the
American Elm.

20. Elm, Chinese
Ulmus parvifolia

Source - China, Korea, Japan
Location - Chateau-sur-Mer, Rosecliff
Height - to 50 ft.   Leaves - to 2 in.

In the warmer sections of its native China and
Japan this elm is an evergreen, whereas with us
it loses its leaves in the winter although keeping
them late in the fall. Small but fast-growing, the
Chinese Elm makes a good ornamental tree with
tiny leaves.

Most elms flower and shed their seed in the
spring; Chinese Elm does so at the other end of
the season, August or September.

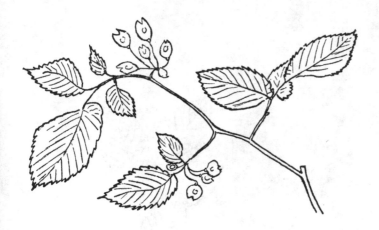

21. Elm, European White - *Ulmus laevis*

Source - Central Europe to Western Asia
Location - Chateau-sur-Mer
Height - to 90 ft.   Leaves - to 5 in.

In many respects the European White Elm resembles the American Elm. Fine points of difference do exist, but it takes a close examination to find them. The flat, disk-like seeds, hanging on thread-like stems, have notches at the top, but they are not as deeply notched as those of the American Elm. The outer edge of each seed disc has a fine margin of fringe. While the lopsided leaves resemble those of American Elms, they run to smaller sizes. The tree itself, on this continent at least, grows far shorter than our native elm.

22. Elm, Scotch - *Ulmus glabra*

Source -
Northern and Central Europe, Western Asia
Location -
The Breakers, Chateau-sur-Mer, Rosecliff
Height - to 120 ft.   Leaves - to 6 1/2 in.

The Scotch Elm occurs less commonly than some
of its varieties. It may be recognized by the rather
large leaves as elm leaves go, which occasionally
end in three points, not just one. The tree goes by
another name, too, the Wych Elm.

As Scottish as the bagpipe is the Camperdown
Elm (*Ulmus glabra camperdowni*), a clonal variety of Scotch Elm from Camperdown, Scotland, and
it is just as individual. This elm, like most unusual
varieties of trees, does not reproduce true to type
from seed. Seed from Camperdown Elms
produces Scotch Elms, not more Camper-
downs. Hence, to reproduce its kind, tree
growers must graft cuttings (called
scions) of it on stems of other trees
(called the stock). They select a
seven or eight foot stock and graft
onto the top. Result - a tree umbrella.

23. Fir, Balsam - *Abies balsamea*

Source - Northern North America
Location - Kingscote
Height - to 70 ft. Needles - 3/4 to 1 in. Cones - to 4 in.

One of the favorite Christmas trees, the Balsam Fir keeps well indoors and gives off the best fragrance on earth. Campers who hit the hay on boughs of balsam will never forget the experience. And anyone can remember the mountain-top splendors by taking home enough twigs to make a balsam pillow. Just strip the needles off and sew them into a small pillow. If you feel like punning, you can letter the pillow with this motto: I pine for thee and balsam too.

Although considered a weed tree by lumber interests, Balsam Fir redeems itself by supplying the clear, liquid balsam of chemists' labs. This forms under numerous blisters on the bark. The narrow outline, dark foliage, blistery bark, and spire-like top characterize Balsam Fir. Its cones, not easily seen from the ground, stand upright on the uppermost twigs.

24. Fir, Douglas - *Pseudotsuga taxifolia*

Source - British Columbia to Texas
Location - Chateau-sur-Mer
Height - to 300 ft.   Needles - 3/4 to 1 1/4 in.
Cones - to 4 1/2 in.

This noteworthy species from the Pacific coast thrives in the rain forests of Oregon, and there the Douglas Fir has become the official state tree. It grows in close ranks, creating dark forest floors where the sunlight never falls. In sheer, magnificent size it yields top honors only to the redwoods.

Douglas Fir combines beauty and utility, being the principal timber tree of the Northwest. It grows fast, has soft, easily-flexed needles and a pleasing, dark green aspect. The hanging cones look shaggy because of three-pronged bracts growing out beyond the cone scales.

The tree takes its name from an admiring explorer, David Douglas, who introduced it to England in 1827.

Sunshine and tree shadows contrast on Rosecliff lawns. Here trees from England, China, Greece, Japan, and Turkey grow congenially.

25. Fir, Greek - *Abies cephalonica*

Source - Greece
Location - Rosecliff
Height - to 100 ft. Needles - to 1 1/4 in. Cones - 6 in.

This uncommon evergreen thrives in its seaside habitat at Rosecliff, where, instead of overlooking the Aegean Sea, it overlooks the Atlantic. The glossy needles display lines of white dots on the undersides, and in full sun pour forth a rich, mellow fragrance. They end in rather sharp points, a feature uncommon among firs. Cones of the Greek Fir stand upright about six inches high.

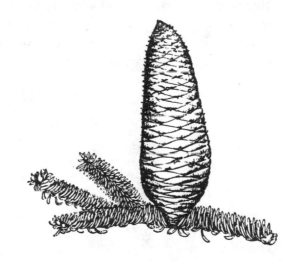

26. Fringetree - *Chionanthus virginicus*

Source - New Jersey, southward and westward
Location - The Breakers, Kingscote
Height - to 10 ft. locally, but higher southward
Leaves - 3 to 6 in.

Victorians liked fringe on their furniture and on
their lawns. This small tree filled the bill outdoors
with its profusion of white, hanging petals in
June. A slow starter in spring, Fringetree waits
for its near relative, the Lilac, to finish blooming.
Then like a June bride it unfurls its white veil.

Native from New Jersey to Florida, Fringetree tolerates New England winters. Europeans
consider it the finest North American exotic. Like
many species of Eastern North American plants,
it curiously has a counterpart in eastern Asia.

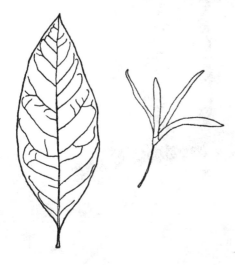

27. Hemlock - *Tsuga canadensis*

Source - Eastern North America
Location - The Breakers, Chateau-sur-Mer
Height - to 110 ft. Needles - to 3/4 in. Cones - to 1 in.

Great hemlocks fell before the axe in former days
when woodsmen sought the rough bark for the
process of tanning hides. With an instrument
called a spud they stripped wide slabs of hemlock
bark and hauled it away to tanneries, while the
naked trunk was left to decay - an ignoble end
to a noble tree.

According to tradition the topmost sprig of a
hemlock always bends to the east, but if you are
lost in the woods, better not count on it.

Given the space to grow in, the weeping form
of Hemlock (*Tsuga canadensis*, variety *pendula*)
spreads outward more than upward. It forms a
mound with one stout trunk at its center. Push
aside the drooping branchlets and step under a
deep shady canopy. Such a tree adorns the grounds
of Chateau-sur-Mer. A far cry from the usually
massive Hemlock of eastern North America, this

is called a sport of that tree. About 1870, according to Donald Wyman in his *Trees for American Gardens*, General Joseph Howland found four Hemlock sports, from which have been propagated all the specimens now grown.

28. Hercules Club - *Aralia spinosa*

Source - Eastern United States
Location - Chateau-sur-Mer, Rosecliff
Height - to 45 ft.   Leaves - to 3 in.

The Hercules of classical myths usually appeared with a spiked club in hand, his weapon against impossible odds. The stems and trunk of this small tree would make a formidable weapon if anyone should ever wield it.

Possibly never deliberately planted on the estates, Hercules club would prove hard to exterminate, as it soon forms colonies of spiny stems. It grows into a flat-topped tree with triply compound, large leaves that give this weed tree a truly exotic look. In late summer clusters of whitish flowers are followed by black-blue berries. Even a weed tree can have something to recommend it.

29. Hickory, Shagbark - *Carya ovata*

Source - Eastern United States
Location - Chateau-sur-Mer
Height - to 120 ft.   Leaves - to 14 in.

It takes more time and patience than most people have to crack a quart of hickory nuts, but the mellow, rich taste makes it worth the while. Cranberry bread with hickory nuts makes a treat par excellence.

Why the shaggy bark? It peels up and down in a way to discourage boys and squirrels from climbing. Like many nut trees the Shagbark Hickory produces nuts wrapped in thick hulls, which, when green, can stain the fingers with a fast dye that won't wash off, but in time it wears off.

Andrew Jackson, or "Old Hickory" (so-called for his tough, enduring nature), lies in his grave beneath six hickories.

30. Holly, English - *Ilex aquifolium*

Source - Southern Europe
Location - The Breakers
Height - to 70 ft.   Leaves - to 3 in.

While few need an introduction to Holly trees, only the specialist can distinguish the many varieties of this species and the others that have been developed since Roman times. In ancient Rome during the winter solstice, celebrated as the Saturnalia, holly helped along the festivities. But holly did not decline and fall with Rome. On the contrary, in one species or another it it is alive and well and native on all continents in the world except Australia and the Poles.

English Holly differs from American (*Ilex opaca*) in its darker, more glossy foliage. The trees at The Breakers display leaves with and without side prickles on the same branches.

American Holly is the state tree of Delaware.

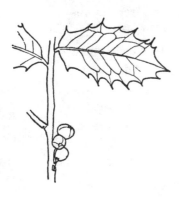

31. Honey Locust, *Gleditsia triacanthos*

Source -
Western New York to Florida and westward
Location - The Breakers, Kingscote
Height - to 135 ft. Leaves 7 to 12 in. Pods 12 to 18 in.

The Honey Locust features what one tree enthusiast calls terrifying thorns, thorns up to four inches long and sometimes double- or triple-pronged. Looking up at the tree, the viewer sees lacy foliage of the compound leaves. At most seasons the long, dark pods hang on, the seeds of which are surrounded by a sweet, honey-like jelly. On some trees the thorns form dense clusters. Boys do not climb Honey Locusts; they find them too standoffish.

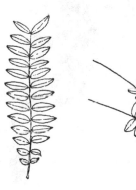

32. Hornbeam, European - *Carpinus betulus*

Source - Europe to Iran
Location - Chateau-sur-Mer
Height - to 70 ft.   Leaves - to 4 in.

Sometimes known as Blue Beach, the Hornbeam attracts attention for its smooth but grooved bark with ridges like muscles in appearance.

Germans planted hedges of Hornbeam saplings close together. When the branches crossed like swords they were scraped at the joint and encouraged to grow into each other, forming eventually an impenetrable, living fence.

So tough and hard is the wood, an axe flung against the Hornbeam's trunk will recoil. This quality made it useful for ox yokes, mauls, and levers.

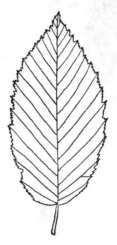

*At Chateau-sur-Mer a Weeping Hemlock (left,
foreground) and a Weeping Beech (center, back-
ground) are two of the many splendid specimens
on this spacious estate.*

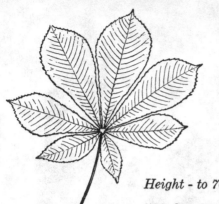

33. Horse Chestnut
Aesculus hippocastanum

Source - the mountains of Greece
Location - The Breakers,
Chateau-sur-Mer, Kingscote,
Marble House, Rosecliff
Height - to 70 ft. Leaves - to 15 in. Seeds - 1 in.

"Under the spreading chestnut tree" is a part of nearly every American's education, and it is thought that Longfellow meant the Horse Chestnut, not the American Chestnut.

Around Narragansett Bay, fishermen catch blackfish (tautog) by this rule of thumb:

When chestnut leaves are big as thumbnail,
Blackfish will bite without fail;
But when the leaves are fully a span,
Try and catch them, if you can.

If you look to this tree for chestnuts to roast and eat, you're barking up the wrong tree. Try instead the American or the Chinese Chestnut. Youngsters gather beautiful horse chestnuts on the way to school in September. Oldsters used to carry them in their pockets to ward off rheumatism.

Horse Chestnut leaves fan out like fingers from the tip of the stem. The tree has one bad habit: its leaves turn brown too early, often in August. When they drop, they leave behind large, sticky buds that look freshly shellacked, and the burs which, on falling, release one of nature's most attractive seeds. The bark of the Horse Chestnut tends to form flakes and scales.

34. Horse Chestnut, Red
Aesculus carnea

Source - hybrid origin, in 1858
Location - Chateau-sur-Mer, Kingscote
Height - to 75 ft. Leaves - to 15 in. Seeds - 1 in.

Take the white flowers of the Horse Chestnut tree and cross them with the red of the Red Buckeye and you come up with the Red Horse Chestnut.

In most plantings the flowering Horse Chestnuts steal the show. If you miss the flowering of either the white or the red - and the white generally comes first - stand beneath the tree and look up at its splayed leaf-fingers. What you lost in flowers, you gained in leaf pattern.

Horticulturists point out that this species resists drought better than the white, which tends to lose its foliage early in a dry season. It has little to add to the fall foliage show, but not much equals the June flowering of the Red Horse Chestnut.

35. Juniper, Pfitzer's
Juniperus chinensis pfitzeriana

Source - China, Mongolia, Japan
Location - The Breakers, The Elms, Kingscote
Height - to 6 ft.

Most often a low shrub, this Juniper takes many different poses. It can become compact or spreading, drooping or erect. As with most junipers, the Pfitzer's has two types of needles - blunt, scaly ones, and sharp, pointed ones. Though it has an informal look, due to its lack of symmetry, Pfitzer's Juniper has become a popular shrub for use in odd corners and along borders.

36. Katsura Tree
Cercidiphyllum japonicum sinense

Source - Central and Western China
Location - The Elms
Height - to 90 ft.   Leaves - to 3 in.

This new-comer to the United States first came to
the Arnold Arboretum at Jamaica Plain, outside
of Boston, Massachusetts, in 1907. In its native
lands it rises out of dense growths of bamboo. The
leaves resemble those of the Redbud tree - Cercis.
Hence the name Cercidiphyllum.

The specimens at The Elms, having been
sheared, stand as dense, erect columns.

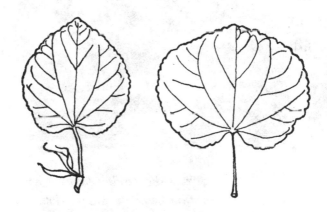

Moving from the glaring summer heat to the deep shade of this Beech at Marble House comes as a welcome relief.

37. Lilac, Amur - *Syringa amurensis*

Source - Manchuria, Northern China
Location - The Elms
Height - to 10 ft.   Leaves - to 4 in.

The Amur Lilac blooms fully a month after the more common dooryard Lilac, winding up its flowering by about the fourth of July. This many-branched shrub produces great heads of bloom in shape like the common Lilac's turrets, wide at the base, narrower at the summit, but always white, and fragrant in the same way Privet is. To most people its fragrance seems cloying. Its strongest asset consists of the timing of its flowers. Most shrubs have set seed when the Amur Lilac blooms.

38. Linden, Bigleaf European
Tilia platyphyllos

Source - Europe
Location -
The Elms, Kingscote, Marble House, Rosecliff
Height - to 100 ft.   Leaves - to 4 in.

The lindens come into glory in early summer when
their myriad white flowers create a world of fragrance. Stand beneath a linden at this time and
hear the bees. With them it is a favorite. They
rifle its flowers for nectar to convert into one of
the most delicious of honeys. Basswood honey of
the roadside stands comes from the American
Linden or Basswood.

Identifying lindens can become confusing,
since most species have heart-shaped leaves and
most are toothed. Even specialists find them a
difficult group. Notice the flowers or seeds. Their
stems sport a leaf-like appendage, called a bract.

39. Linden, Crimean - *Tilia euchlora*

Source - hybrid
Location - The Breakers, Rosecliff
Height - to 60 ft.   Leaves - to 4 in.

The glossy leaves of Crimean Linden give the
tree a distinct appearance all summer, and at any
season the smooth, yellow-green twigs are a give-
away. It shares the family trait of having highly
fragrant blossoms, and serves well as a graceful
shade tree. Besides that, it withstands drought
well.

This and other lindens go by the name, limes.

40. Linden, Littleleaf European
Tilia cordata

Source - Europe
Location - The Breakers, Chateau-sur-Mer,
The Elms, Marble House, Rosecliff
Height - to 100 ft.   Leaves - to 2 1/2 in.

In Estonia and other European countries, housewives brew a fine tea of linden blossoms. The recipe: snip off the newly opened blossoms in any quantity desired; cure in warm sunlight under cover of paper; when thoroughly dry, pack away in tightly closed jars. To brew the tea, steep the fresh or dried blossoms in hot water, as in brewing regular tea, add lemon and sugar if desired, and enjoy your linden tea.

41. Linden, Silver - *Tilia tomentosa*

Source - Southeastern Europe, Western Asia
Location - The Elms, Marble House
Height - to 90 ft.   Leaves - to 4 in.

Although the other Lindens seem all too similar and difficult to tell apart, this one presents no problems. The leaves, coated with fine, silver-white down on the undersides, put the Silver Linden in a class by itself. When the wind ripples those leaves, the viewer sees a two-toned silver and green effect not often encountered. Its compact habit of growth makes the Silver Linden look sheared.

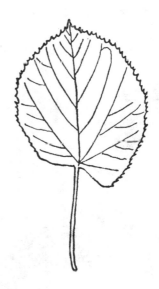

42. Magnolia, Saucer
Magnolia soulangeana

*Source - a hybrid from the garden of Etienne
Soulange-Bodin near Paris in the 1820s*
Location - Kingscote
Height - to 25 ft.   Leaves - to 8 in.

Most people think of this species when magnolias
are mentioned. A tree from which many forms
have come, the Saucer Magnolia usually has petals
of rose-purple on the outside, and white or pale
rose within. The flowers give full measure of satis-
faction, because they bloom before the leaves un-
fold to obscure them. Occasionally a tree will put on
a second show in late summer when a few flowers
open, but they are smaller and leaf-hidden. The
tree's finest hour is in May.

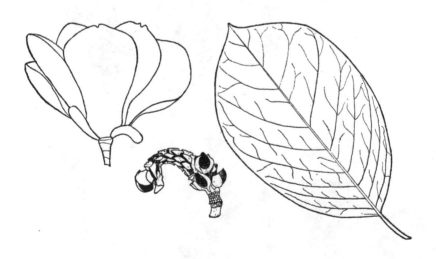

43. Magnolia, Yulan - *Magnolia denudata*

Source - Central China
Location - Chateau-sur-Mer
Height - to 45 ft.   Leaves - to 6 in.

Cultivated as early as the year 627 A. D. during
the Tang dynasty in China, the Yulan Magnolia
has stood for candor and beauty. Its creamy white
petals adorn the tree in late April and early May
before the leaves appear.

More often than not, magnolias are planted in
open spaces where their beauty may be viewed
from all angles. They frequently combine fragrance
and beauty. The genus takes its name from a
French botanist, Pierre Magnol.

Magnolias suffer from transplanting. Special
care must be taken to protect their tender roots.

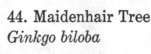

44. Maidenhair Tree
Ginkgo biloba

Source - Eastern China
Location - The Breakers,
Chateau-sur-Mer, The Elms, Kingscote
Height - to 120 ft. Leaves - to 4 in. fruit - 3/4 in.

This tree has come to us unaltered straight from the age of dinosaurs. Called a living fossil by Darwin, it may be found imprinted as a fossil in rocks over a million years old, while it thrives today in cities the world over.

Ginkgos owe their very existence to the fact that Chinese priests of the tenth century rescued a few specimens of the nearly extinct tree to raise on their temple grounds. Buddhists carried it from China to Japan, and later travelers transported it to all points east and west. It appeared in this country in 1784. Yet in China, where this tree migration all started, not a single specimen is known to grow in the wild. (In this it resembles the Franklinia, which was found once and collected by the Bartrams in Georgia but has never again been seen in the wild.) Except for human efforts the Ginkgo would probably have succumbed to the evolutionary process of elimination.

Ginkgo trees improve with age. City dust and fumes discourage them not a bit. The yellow, cherry-like fruit of female trees gives the tree a bad name because of its foul odor when ripe. But plant the male tree, and you'll have a column of green fans waving at you all summer long and gold ones in the fall. Approach your Ginkgo Tree with respect!

45. Maple, Amur - *Acer ginnala*

Source - Manchuria, North China, Japan
Location - Kingscote
Height - to 20 ft. Leaves - 1 to 4 in.

If the Amur Maple qualifies as a tree at all, it must be as a dwarf. Its chief attraction consists of the winged seeds. The wings themselves are nearly parallel, turning a bright red promptly and hanging on for weeks against the rich green foliage. Its yellow-green, clustered flowers in early June possess a sweet fragrance which attracts hordes of bees and other small insects.

Ernest "Chinese" Wilson tells us that the leaves of Amur Maple had a considerable economic importance in Korea, where they were gathered in late summer and after being dried in the sun, were packed in bales for export to China. The Chinese prepared blue, black, and khaki-colored dyes from them.

46. Maple Fullmoon - *Acer japonicum*

Source - Japan
Location - The Breakers, Kingscote
Height - to 40 ft.   Leaves - to 5 in.

The name, Fullmoon, alludes to the nearly round outline of the leaves of this maple. A choice tree from Japan, the Fullmoon Maple seldom becomes massive in size, but spreads its graceful, bright green foliage at heights where it can be easily viewed. The leaves grow precisely opposite each other along the stems. Like most maples, it flowers and sets seed early in the season, and gets on with the business of nurturing buds for next year's blossoms and leaves.

47. Maple, Japanese
Acer palmatum

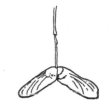

Source - Japan
Location - The Breakers,
Chateau-sur-Mer, The Elms, Kingscote
Height - to 20 ft. Leaves - to 5 in. Seeds - to 2 in.

Americans forever associate cherry trees with
Japan, yet to the Japanese, maples figure pro-
minently. A traveler in old Japan described a fall
jubilee, when families walked about, viewing the
many forms of Maple in ruby-colored foliage, just
as city people in this country head for the mountains at foliage time. This low, ornamental tree
will never set a whole hillside ablaze with color
as the Sugar Maple does, but certain forms display a lively red from the start of the season to
the glorious finish.

As a species, the Japanese Maple varies its leaf
pattern in degree of intricacy, and some forms
are not red at all but green. Seedlings usually fail
to grow true to their parent stock.

At Chateau-sur-Mer varieties occur with very
deeply cut leaves and narrow segments, these varieties having both dark red and green foliage.

48. Maple, Norway - *Acer platanoides*

Source - Europe, Western Asia
Location - The Breakers, Chateau-sur-Mer,
The Elms, Kingscote, Marble House, Rosecliff
Height - to 70 ft. Leaves - 8 in. Seeds - 2 1/2 in. wide

The city of Newport contains almost no native trees. Norway Maple, not native, but introduced from Europe, multiplies freely, and on this island, which is a melting pot of trees, it has readily become naturalized. It serves well along busy streets, seemingly tolerant of dirt and smoke. Copious seeds insure a steady increase of these maples, and despite the many seeds the squirrels eat, they do their share of reforestation, planting hordes of them along hedgerows and in vacant lands. The Norway Maple coming up in your own back yard may well be a living memorial to a departed squirrel.

To be sure you have a specimen of Norway Maple and not the similar Sugar Maple, break off a leaf stalk or a new, green stem. If it bleeds white, sticky sap, it's Norway Maple. At The Breakers grows a special type of Norway Maple known for its dark red foliage (*Acer platanoides rubrum*).

*Formal shrubs and informal trees blend at
The Elms, where the last American Elm has
sadly succumbed to disease.*

49. Maple, Silver
Acer saccharinum

Source - Eastern North America
Location - Chateau-sur-Mer,
The Elms, Kingscote, Marble House
Height - to 60 ft.   Leaves - to 8 in.
Seeds - to 3 in. wide

Call the Silver Maple the tree in a hurry. Even
during a January thaw its buds may swell per-
ceptibly. Before the Spring Equinox, it has swol-
len to the bursting point. Unlike most maples,
and in fact unlike most other trees, its seeds go
right to work and sprout the same season - opera-
tion headstart in action.

This native of eastern North America has airy,
graceful leaves with silvery, white undersides.
When they flutter in the wind, a pleasing contrast
results. Generations of weather prophets have be-
lieved that when the undersides of maple leaves
show on a summer day, rain will be forthcoming.
Often they're right, and the explanation lies in
the fact that an increase of moisture in the air
preceding a storm tends to twist the leaf stalks.
Science in this case agrees with what the weather-
wise have known all along.

50. Maple, Sugar
Acer saccharum

Source - Eastern North America
Location - The Breakers,
Chateau-sur-Mer, Kingscote
Height - to 120 ft.   Leaves - to 6 in. long

What other tree forms the basis for a tourist trade? Thousands migrate northward in foliage time - usually the second week in October in New England - to see this king of color trees. Those who find it at its peak come away with one word for the Sugar Maple - indescribable. Nor is that all. As syrup its sap has flavor par excellence.

Foresters recently cruised our woods, eyeing Sugar Maples for timber to export to Japan for bowling alleys. Curly and bird's-eye forms make ideal wood for outstanding furniture. An old-time woodsman, when asked if he could predict which trees would produce the choice curly grain by the sprouts up and down the trunk, shook his head no. "I put no more stock in that than in last year's bird nest."

Sugar Maple has become the state tree of New York, Vermont, West Virginia, and Wisconsin.

51. Maple, Sycamore
Acer pseudo-platanus

Source - Europe and Western Asia
Location - The Breakers, Chateau-sur-Mer,
The Elms, Kingscote, Marble House, Rosecliff
Height - to 70 ft.   Leaves - to 7 in.
Seeds - to 3 in. wide

If anyone questions the value of botanical names
for plants and trees, let him consider the common
name for this tree. Maple - yes. But Sycamore?
That, authorities claim, belongs to one tree only, the
Fig Tree, which the biblical Zacchaeus climbed to
see his Master. Just as pansies stand for thoughts,
and rosemary for remembrance, so the Sycamore
Maple through a mixed-up association with Zacchaeus has come to stand for curiosity.

Despite the name, this tree has a very real identity. The principal hardwood tree of Europe, it
has scaly bark (admittedly like the Sycamore or
Buttonwood), deeply veined leaves and chains of
hanging blossoms. Seaports like Newport formerly
used the Sycamore Maple near the ocean, as it suf-
fers but little from salt spray. Against tempests
spawned at sea it is a strong first line of defense.

52. Mountain Ash, European
Sorbus aucuparia

Source - Europe to Western Asia
Location - The Breakers, Chateau-sur-Mer
Height - to 45 ft. Leaves - to 7 in.

A tree of the craggy hills of Europe, where it grows
in straightened circumstances, the Mountain Ash,
or Rowantree, improves under cultivation. Its
mute green foliage recommends it all summer
long, but the heads of orange fruit attract attention in fall and well into winter, if the birds don't
get to them first.

The Mountain Ash has entered the folklore of
Europe as a tree to exorcise evil spirits and undo
their work.

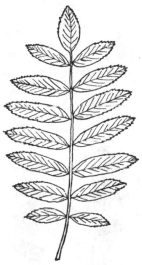

53. Mulberry, White - *Morus alba*

Source - China
Location - The Elms, Kingscote, Rosecliff
Height - to 50 ft. Leaves - 5 in. Fruit to 1 1/2 in.

The White Mulberry has become as much a part of civilization as the cat. Its use in making silk goes back to pre-history. Finicky silkworms prefer Morus alba to any other species of mulberry. The tree is no new-comer to Rhode Island, having been brought here by French Huguenot settlers in the 1680s.

Mulberry leaves take many forms. Some are heart-shaped and symmetrical, others irregularly lobed. Birds indulge in eating the pulpy fruit immoderately, so much so, in fact, that farmers who wanted their cherry crop to themselves used to plant mulberries alongside the Cherry trees. This enticed the birds away from the more desirable cherries.

The weeping form (*Morus alba pendula*) seldom gets above ten feet high. It droops, but otherwise it has the same characteristics as the species.

54. Oak, English - *Quercus robur*

Source - Europe, North Africa, Western Asia
Location - The Breakers, Chateau-sur-Mer,
Kingscote, Marble House
Height - to 120 ft.   Leaves - 2 to 5 in.

Known for longevity, the English Oaks in Sherwood Forest shaded Robin Hood and Long John. English Oak went into the construction of St. Paul's Cathedral, and it supplied first-rate timber for the British Navy of "Good Queen Bess's" day. The only native oak in the British Isles, it is nevertheless distributed in North Africa and Western Asia. Here in Newport County, especially in Newport and Jamestown, this oak has become naturalized, no doubt with the aid of forgetful squirrels.

English Oak belongs to the White Oak group which features leaves with rounded lobes minus bristle tips.

55. Oak, Pin - *Quercus palustris*

Source - Central and Eastern United States
Location - The Breakers, Chateau-sur-Mer
Height - to 75 ft.   Leaves - 3 to 4 3/4 in.

Growing naturally on moist ground, along rivers and ponds, the Pin Oak nevertheless takes easily to upland parks and roadsides. From its thick central trunk grow many small branches in a distinct pattern. That is, the lower branches droop noticeably, the middle ones tend to grow out straight, while the upper ones reach for the sun. So it resembles a calisthenics diagram of a figure with arms extended upward, outward, and down.

Numerous little twigs like spurs earn the name Pin Oak. The low, flattish acorns take two years to mature.

56. Oak, Red
Quercus borealis

Source - Eastern North America
Location - Kingscote
Height - to 150 ft.   Leaves - 5 to 9 in.

New Jersey has adopted the Red Oak as its state
tree. Because the Red Oak grows so commonly in
our forests, its value as an ornamental has been
overlooked here, but not in Europe where it is the
prize American Oak. Fast growing, it soon develops a columnar trunk.

Of the two groups of oaks, this species belongs
to the Black Oak group. Its leaves end in sharp
points or bristles.

The saw mill operator sees a beautiful sight
when his saw rifts a log of Red Oak. The deep pink
wood, still damp from the forest, reveals a wide-
patterned grain of long ellipses or wish-bones,
with lighter and darker highlights.

57. Oak, Sargent's - *Quercus sargenti*

Source - Hybrid, possibly Sargent's, which is a
cross of Quercus montana with Quercus robur
Location - The Elms
Height - to 50 ft.   Leaves - to 8 in.

Little can be learned about this puzzling oak. Its
identity remains a secret, hence it must be enjoyed
for what it is, a low, wide-spreading tree with
neatly toothed leaves. Perhaps the best compli-
ment to pay it is to say that it is one of a kind.
Sargent's Oak, if such it is, stands at the parking
lot of The Elms.

Alfred Rehder, whose work, *Manual of Culti-*
vated Trees and Shrubs, has been the classic in its
field since 1927, first described Quercus sargenti.

58. Oak, Turkey - *Quercus cerris*

Source - Southeastern Europe and Western Asia
Location - Chateau-sur-Mer, The Elms,
Marble House, Rosecliff
Height - to 120 ft.   Leaves - to 4 in.

In its native lands this oak reaches great heights,
and there, as elsewhere, it serves many and odd
purposes. The English prefer Turkey Oak for
wainscoating. The tree has been introduced in
South Africa and is planted there to discourage
the growth of grasses, where grass fires pose a
threat annually. On the Newport estates the oak
grows to fine proportions, making a handsome
shade tree. The small leaves look ornamental, and
the acorns are enclosed in cups bristling with
curved and twisted points.

59. Pine, Japanese Black - *Pinus thunbergi*

Source - Japan
Location - Rosecliff, The Elms
Height - to 90 ft. Needles - to 5 in. and 2 per bundle

Japanese Black Pine finds favor in seaside gardens where it can withstand strong winds and salt spray. Hence it is well suited to its situation at Rosecliff. If it lacks the symmetry of some other pines, its contortions lend an oriental aspect to the tree which the Japanese use to good advantage.

The pine takes its species name from the Swedish botanist Carl Peter Thunberg.

Plantings of Japanese Black Pine in Newport and Little Compton, Rhode Island, produce some of the finest specimens in Eastern North America.

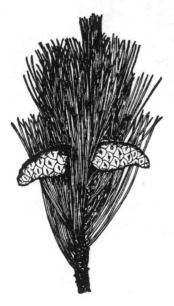

60. Plane Tree, London
Platanus acerifolia

Source - hybrid origin, before 1700
Location - The Breakers, Chateau-sur-Mer,
The Elms, Kingscote, Marble House, Rosecliff
Height - to 100 ft. Leaves - to 10 in. Seeds - 1 in.

In Rhode Island and wherever the London Plane
Trees or their next of kin, the Sycamores, occur,
there are giants in the land, for these trees grow
not just tall, but massive. The American Forestry
Association publishes a "Social Register of Big
Trees" in which it records a Sycamore measuring
80 feet high, 32 feet, ten inches in circumference,
with a spread of 102 feet. For diameter of a tree
divide the circumference by Pi, roughly by 3. Circumference is not measured at the ground level
but 4 1/2 feet up.

Besides the flaking, mottled bark, which is ob-
vious, and the cherry-sized, button-like seeds
hanging on all winter, notice the base of the leaf-
stalk. It entirely surrounds the new bud, not the
usual setup in tree buds.

Dickens set a chapter of his *A Tale of Two Cities*
under a London Plane Tree, using its implied sta-
bility to contrast with the turbulence in the other
city of the story, Paris.

61. Rhododendron Hybrid

Source - North America and Asia
Location - The Elms, Kingscote, Marble House
Height - to 35 ft.   Leaves - to 8 in.

Many hybrid varieties of Rhododendron trace their
parentage to *Rhododendron maximum*, native to
the Eastern United States, including Rhode Island,
where it sometimes passes under the name Deer
Laurel. In shaded locations the leaves may hang
on for seven or eight years. Count them - a year
for each whorl, beginning at the bud. Recoiling
against subfreezing temperatures, the leaves char-
acteristically roll up and resemble green cigars.
But come a thaw, and they uncoil unharmed.

Is Rhododendron a tree or a shrub? When a
root sends up many shoots, none of which takes
the lead, and none rises higher than twenty feet,
botanists consider it a shrub.

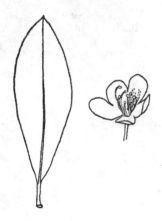

A bold pattern of Horse Chestnut leaves shades the driveway at Kingscote, and Japanese Maples carry out the design.

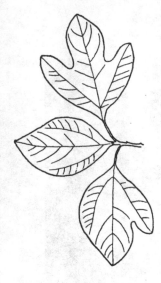

62. Sassafras - *Sassafras albidum*

Source - Eastern United States
Location - Rosecliff
Height - to 60 ft.   Leaves - to 6 in.

The Sassafras with its three types of leaves on the same branch makes tree enthusiasts of youngsters. The leaves come in plain ovals, or with one thumb like a mitten, or with two thumbs on the same leaf.

The fragrance of Sassafras extends from the leaves through the green twigs to the aged bark and the very roots. Settlers in North America eagerly sought the tree to send back to Europe.

Oil of Sassafras finds its way into gum drops and homemade soap. For sassafras tea pull roots of the young sprouts, break off at the ground level, discarding any part above ground, as it will taste too strong. Five or six roots about the size of your fingers will make a quart of tea. Steep the roots fifteen or twenty minutes. Add lemon and sugar.

63. Scholar Tree, Chinese
Sophora japonica

Source - China and Korea
Location - Chateau-sur-Mer, Rosecliff
Height - to 75 ft.   Leaves - to 9 in.

To the Chinese - the Scholar Tree; to the Japanese - Pagoda Tree. This native of China and Korea moved to Japan with the Japanese and has been cultivated by them for over a thousand years. It deserves to be. It serves as a good shade tree, has few pests, if any, but best of all, it blooms in August past the midpoint of the growing season when most other flowering trees have long since gone to seed. On green twigs, the Scholar Tree puts forth clusters of creamy-white, pea-shaped flowers, not unlike Wistaria or Acacia. The pods, legumes, are constricted in the middle giving them a wasp-waist appearance.

A weeping specimen (*Sophora japonica pendula*) grows at Chateau-sur-Mer in addition to the upright tree.

64. Silverbell - *Halesia carolina*

Source - Southeastern United States
Location - Chateau-sur-Mer, The Elms
Height - to 30 ft. Leaves - to 7 in.

A second name for the Silverbell, Snowdrop Tree,
gives a truer picture of it in bloom. Spring hangs
the clear white ornaments on it in groups of two
to five just about when the dogwoods flower. If
you miss the flowering, you can still enjoy the odd,
pointed seed pods with their four ridges or wings.
If you were to slice a twig with a knife, you would
find the pith divided into tiny chambers. Silverbell is a Southern belle by nature, but transplants
easily in the North. Its name honors Stephen
Hales (1677 - 1761), author of a work on *Vegetable
Staticks* which is concerned with the loss of water
in plants, rate of growth, etc.

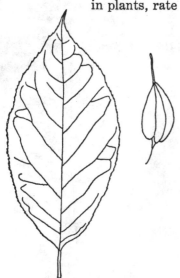

65. Sourwood - *Oxydendron arboreum*

Source - Southeastern United States
Location - The Elms
Height - to 50 ft.   Leaves - to 6 in.

The Heath Family, which claims Sourwood as a distinguished member, is an easy favorite with outdoor people. In this country one of the lowest Heaths is the cranberry and the tallest is Sourwood, with blueberries, laurel, azaleas, rhododendron, and many others in between. Another name for Sourwood, the Lily-of-the-valley-tree, refers to the slender fingers of prim, white flowers that come out in mid-season. And the bees are ready for it, since from its nectar they manufacture honey considered second to none.

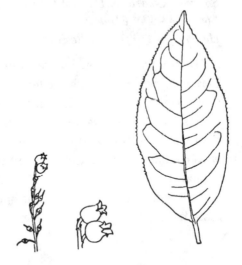

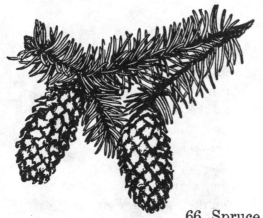

66. Spruce, Colorado
Picea pungens glauca

Source - Colorado, Utah, Wyoming, New Mexico
Location - The Elms
Height - to 150 ft. Needles - to 1 in. Cones - to 4 in.

A favorite tree of suburbanites, Colorado or Blue
Spruce turns up beside split-level houses, Cape
Cod cottages, even mobile homes! The many varieties, blue, glaucous, and silvery, show their
colors early in life, and hence can be purchased
with confidence in what lies ahead for this neat,
formal, touch-me-not tree.

Colorado and Utah honor this spruce as their
state tree.

67. Spruce, Norway - *Picea abies*

Source - Europe
Location - The Breakers, The Elms, Kingscote
Height - to 90 ft. Needles - to 3/4 in. Cones to 6 in.

A Victorian favorite, this tree stands guard over
countless country cemeteries in northeastern
America, and for that reason has earned the nick-
name Graveyard Spruce. Thanks to itinerant
peddlars it became widely distributed. The dark,
somber-looking sentinel serves well singly in
parks, or in rows as windbreaks. Norway Spruce
supplies much timber to Europe. It produces
crops of tan cones six inches long, with
glossy and stiff scales.

68. Spruce, Sakhalin - *Picea Glehni*

Source - Sakhalin Island
Location - The Breakers
Height - to 120 ft. Needles - to 1/2 in. Cones to 3 in.

The Sakhalin Spruce, a relative newcomer among cultivated trees on this continent, made its appearance at the Arnold Arboretum in 1894. A Russian botanist named Friedrich Schmidt had first collected seed of the tree on Sakhalin Island north of Japan.

This slow-growing spruce forms a compact pyramid in outline, having very short, blunt needles that catch the eye with their dark green but shiny aspect. Rare in cultivation, it is seldom offered for sale by nurserymen. To date, the Sakhalin Spruce has been found growing at only one other location in Newport.

69. Spruce, White - *Picea glauca*

Source - Northern North America
Location - Chateau-sur-Mer
Height - to 90 ft. Needles - to 3/4 in. Cones - to 2 in.

In all probability the paper you are now looking at came from pulp of this species of spruce, which abounds in the northern United States and Canada. Paper companies own thousand-acre tracts of White Spruce. When you use recycled paper you are helping to keep one more spruce tree alive.

As a lawn tree, White Spruce holds its own, being generally conical or pyramidal in outline, neat and thrifty - spruced up - able to withstand strong winds and rigorous winters. White Spruce has one bad habit, but you could live next to it for years without noticing it - the disagreeable scent of its foliage when crushed. Lumber Jacks call it Skunk Spruce.

70. Sweetgum - *Liquidambar styraciflua*

Source - Southeastern United States
Location - The Breakers, Chateau-sur-Mer,
The Elms, Kingscote, Marble House
Height - to 120 ft.   Leaves - to 6 in.   Seeds - 1 in.

Any tree that can supply wood for railroad ties
or butter dishes or television cabinets must have
something special about it. And it has. Sweetgum
is a tree for all seasons. In the winter the branches
of most (but not all) specimens show distinctive
corky ridges. What was nature thinking of when
she made these? Spring finds the tree alive with
a sweet gum, for which Linnaeus, the father of
botany, gave the tree its generic name. The star-
shaped leaves of summer take on a wine-crimson
coloring in autumn, and once they fall off, they
leave behind sharp-pronged globes, the seed con-
tainers, that hang on until makers of dry floral
arrangements need them at Christmas time.

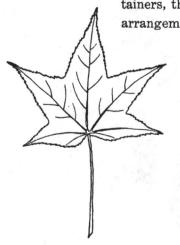

71. Tulip Tree
Liriodendron tulipifera

Source - Eastern United States
Location - Chateau-sur-Mer, Rosecliff
Height - to 180 ft.   Leaves - to 6 in.

The woodworker may call this tree
Tulip Poplar or Whitewood. He
values it for the greenish, fine wood
for furniture, shelves, breadboards.

If the word stately applies to any tree at
all, it surely applies to the Tulip Tree. It forms
massive trunks that shoot straight for the sky. It
often ascends twenty feet without a single branch.
Related to the magnolias, the Tulip Tree flowers
out in showy yellow-orange-green blossoms, only
slightly resembling tulips. Buds and twigs have a
pungent aroma. Don't miss the leaf pattern and
the thick texture.

Kentucky calls this species its state tree, and
so do Tennessee, North Carolina, and Indiana. A
precocious tree anywhere, it surmounts the oaks
and maples of the hardwood forest - leaves them
behind in its straight ascent for heaven.

72. English Walnut - *Juglans regia*

Source - Southeastern Europe, Himalayas, China
Location - Chateau-sur-Mer
Height - to 90 ft.   Leaves - to 30 in.

This nut tree originated in Asia, although it came
to this country by way of England. Hence the
name English Walnut. Walnuts bought at the
market, either in or out of their shells, are generally of this species, their shells being somewhat
sculptured, but with an overall smooth surface.
California, Oregon, and Washington grow the
English Walnut commercially.

The tough wood of this (and other) species
makes good furniture and gun stocks.

If you raise an English Walnut in hopes of an
annual feast of nuts, you'll first have to outwit
the squirrel. He won't sleep nights if he knows
about your nut tree.

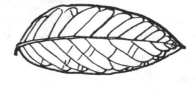

73. Willow, Weeping - *Salix babylonica*

Source - China
Location - Kingscote
Height - to 30 ft.   Leaves - to 6 in.

The father of Botany, Linnaeus, gave to this tree
the specific name *babylonica*. But it seems to have
originated not there, but in China, and possibly
was carried from there to the Mediterranean along
the old overland trade route.

According to one account, when Napoleon was
exiled to St. Helena, he sat under a Weeping Willow for days on end, remembering better days.
Hero worshippers thereafter sought shoots from
that tree, and Napoleon Willows were planted
throughout the Western World.

The drooping twigs of Weeping Willow trees
respond to the first touch of spring by turning
vivid yellow. The trees flower early and produce
myriads of slender, pointed leaves that add to
the weeping effect.

74. Yew - *Taxus baccata*

Source - Europe, Northern Africa, Western Asia
Location - The Breakers, Chateau-sur-Mer,
The Elms, Kingscote, Rosecliff
Height - to 50 ft. Needles - to 1 in. Berries - 1/2 in.

The English Yew and the Japanese (*Taxus cuspidata*) take many forms. One form, the Irish Yew, grows stiffly straight. It was first found growing on a mountainside in Ireland, and all the present specimens derive from cuttings from that original source. Dark and formal, yews suit a wide variety of situations. They can even be cut as a hedge.

In past centuries Yew provided the most desirable wood for highly flexible bows in archery.

The seed of the Yew berry is poisonous, but the pulp surrounding it is not. Furthermore, the needles when green are non-poisonous, but on drying, they become harmful.

As with the hollies, Yew trees are either male or female, hence they do not all bear berries. But the berries are of a soft, raspberry red color.

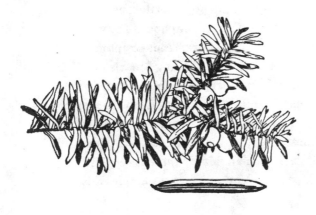

Trees listed by the Estates
on which they appear

The Breakers

Arborvitae. Ash, European. Beech, European.
Birch, European. Cedar, Atlas. Cryptomeria.
Cypress, Bald. Cypress, Hinoki. Cypress, Sawara.
Elm, Scotch. Fringetree. Hemlock. Holly, English.
Honey Locust. Horse Chestnut. Juniper, Pfitzer's.
Linden, Crimean. Linden, Littleleaf European.
Maidenhair Tree (Ginkgo). Maple, Fullmoon.
Maple, Japanese. Maple, Norway. Maple, Sugar.
Maple, Sycamore. Mountain Ash. Oak, English.
Oak, Pin. Plane Tree, London. Spruce, Norway.
Spruce, Sakhalin. Sweetgum. Yew.

Chateau-sur-Mer

Arborvitae. Ash, European. Beech, European.
Birch, Paper. Box. Buckeye, Bottlebrush.
Cherry, Cornelian. Cherry, Japanese Flowering.
Coffee Tree, Kentucky. Cork Tree. Cryptomeria.
Cypress, Hinoki. Dogwood. Elm, American.
Elm, Chinese. Elm, European White. Elm, Scotch.
Fir, Douglas. Hemlock. Hercules Club. Hickory,
Shagbark. Hornbeam, European. Horse Chestnut.
Horse Chestnut, Red. Linden, Littleleaf Euro-
pean. Magnolia, Yulan. Maidenhair Tree (Ginkgo).
Maple, Japanese. Maple, Norway. Maple, Silver.

Maple, Sugar. Maple, Sycamore. Mountain Ash.
Oak, English. Oak, Pin. Oak, Turkey. Plane
Tree, London. Scholar Tree, Chinese. Silverbell.
Spruce, White. Sweetgum. Tulip Tree. Walnut,
English. Yew.

The Elms

Arborvitae. Beech, European. Box. Cypress, Hi-
noki. Cypress, Sawara. Dogwood. Horse Chestnut.
Juniper, Pfitzer's. Katsura Tree. Lilac, Amur.
Linden, Bigleaf European. Linden, Littleleaf Eu-
ropean. Linden, Silver. Maidenhair Tree (Ginkgo).
Maple, Japanese. Maple, Norway. Maple, Silver.
Maple, Sycamore. Mulberry, White. Oak, English.
Oak, Pin. Oak, Sargent's. Oak, Turkey. Pine, Ja-
panese Black. Plane Tree, London. Rhododendron.
Silverbell. Sourwood. Spruce, Colorado. Spruce,
Norway. Sweetgum. Yew.

Kingscote

Beech, European. Birch, Paper. Box. Cherry,
Japanese Flowering. Cherry, Sweet. Cypress,
Sawara. Dogwood. Elm, American. Fir, Balsam.
Fringetree. Honey Locust. Horse Chestnut. Horse
Chestnut, Red. Juniper, Pfitzer's. Linden, Big-
leaf European. Magnolia, Saucer. Maidenhair Tree
(Ginkgo). Maple, Amur. Maple, Fullmoon. Maple,
Japanese. Maple, Norway. Maple, Silver. Maple,

Sugar. Maple, Sycamore. Mulberry, White. Oak,
English. Oak, Red. Plane Tree, London. Rhodo-
dendron. Spruce, Norway. Sweetgum. Willow,
Weeping. Yew.

Marble House

Beech, European. Cryptomeria. Elm, American.
Elm, Scotch. Horse Chestnut. Linden, Littleleaf
European. Linden, Silver. Maple, Norway. Maple,
Silver. Maple, Sycamore. Oak, English. Oak, Tur-
key. Plane Tree, London. Rhododendron. Sweet-
gum.

Rosecliff

Beech, European. Box. Elm, Chinese. Elm, Scotch.
Fir, Greek. Hercules Club. Horse Chestnut.
Linden, Crimean. Linden, Littleleaf European.
Maple, Norway. Maple, Sycamore. Mulberry,
White. Oak, Turkey. Pine, Japanese Black. Plane
Tree, London. Sassafras. Scholar Tree, Chinese.
Tulip Tree. Yew.

Special acknowledgment is due for the use of illustrations from: Arthur T. Viertel's *Trees, Shrubs,
and Vines*, State University College of Forestry
at Syracuse University, 1961; U. S. Department
of Agriculture - 1949 *Yearbook of Agriculture;*
Liberty H. Bailey's *The Cultivated Evergreens*,
New York, Macmillan, 1923; Alfred C. Hottes' *The
Book of Trees*, New York, The A. T. De La Mare
Company, Inc., 1932; Charles S. Sargent's *Manual
of the Trees of North America*, Boston, Houghton
Mifflin, 1922. The illustrations for Species Nos.
21, 57, 58, 68, and 69 were drawn by the author.
The photographs of the estates were taken by
John T. Hopf.

500 copies of this book were designed, hand set,
and printed at The Third & Elm Press, Newport,
Rhode Island. This is a reproduction of the original
edition.

CPSIA information can be obtained
at www.ICGtesting.com
Printed in the USA
JSHW041455110122
21944JS00001B/11